THE HEART SUTRA

the Prajna Paramita

THE HEART SUTRA

the Prajna Paramita

With an introduction by Pamela Bloom

FRIEDMAN/FAIRFAX
PUBLISHERS

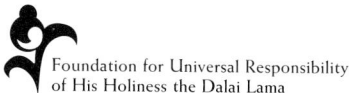

Foundation for Universal Responsibility
of His Holiness the Dalai Lama

A FRIEDMAN/FAIRFAX BOOK
FRIEDMAN/FAIRFAX PUBLISHERS

Please visit our website: www.metrobooks.com

This edition published by Friedman/Fairfax by arrangement with
David Alexander Publishing & Full Circle

2002 Friedman/Fairfax Publishers

ISBN 1-58663-717-7

Created by David Alexander Publishing
Designed by The Bridgewater Book Company

All rights reserved. No part of this publication may be reproduced,
or utilized in any form or by any means,
electronic or mechanical, without prior permission in writing from the publisher.

Distributed by Sterling Publishing Company, Inc.
387 Park Avenue South
New York, NY 10016

Distributed in Canada by Sterling Publishing
Canadian Manda Group
One Atlantic Avenue, Suite 105
Toronto, Ontario, Canada M6K 3E7

Printed in Singapore

Contents

INTRODUCING THE HEART SUTRA

6

THE HEART SUTRA

14

Introducing the Heart Sutra

If you visit a Zen or Tibetan Buddhist monastery today, you will most probably hear the sonorous, deeply provocative chanting of the Heart Sutra. It is the shortest and most popular sutra, or teaching, in Buddhism—regarded as the very essence of the Buddha's enlightened mind.

Most probably composed by visionary monks in South India between 100 BCE and 100 CE, the Heart Sutra is part of an oral tradition known as The Perfection of Wisdom (or Prajna Paramita), that dates back to the era (four centuries earlier) of the historical Buddha himself. In fact it has been postulated that Shakyamuni Buddha chose to hide these teachings from the world until such time that beings were evolved enough to hear them without danger.

As an essential text of the Mahayana School of Buddhism, the Prajna Paramita has contained as many as 100,000 lines but also as few as 300 lines (in the Diamond Sutra) and 14 in the Heart Sutra.

The translation provided here focuses on the Heart Sutra's absolute essence. That His Holiness the Dalai Lama chose this sutra as the last prayer he chanted before escaping Tibet in 1959 shows its inspirational power. As in the original, the text includes one of the most beloved mantras in Buddhism.

THE HEART SUTRA

Seemingly full of contradictions, the Heart Sutra is truly a poetry of dialectics. Although monks and scholars, especially Tibetans, have passionately debated its tenets for centuries, it is said that its full meaning can never be fully grasped by the intellectual mind.

Rather, it is only through the intuitive, meditative mind that one can penetrate the Heart Sutra's mysteries—a realm where paradox, nonduality and unknowability run free. The magic of this teaching lies in the oneness between its process and content; it is as much a proclamation of enlightenment as it is a guide or mind map for realizing it. In recent years, as this text was disseminated to the West, it gained an undeserved reputation for nihilism. On the contrary, according to the Buddhist teachings, the Heart Sutra is absolute cause for rejoicing—the good news that there is no solid self on which anything of permanent ground can be constructed.

Since, as the Buddha purported, the concept of a separate, permanent self, is the cause of suffering, introduction to the state of mind that embraces no-self is surely the cause of ultimate liberation.

But how can we, Westerners, so firmly attached to the ideals of individualism and materialism, ever begin to understand this viewpoint…that is so shocking, so mystical, so revolutionary?

Seen in its entirety, the Heart Sutra is actually a feisty dialogue between two monks who have gathered with hundreds of

THE HEART SUTRA

their colleagues in the presence of the Buddha to receive his teachings. The location is Vulture Peak, a mountain in Rajgir, a place that is visitable today in modern Bihar. What is most remarkable about this auspicious moment is that the Buddha, as divine teacher, utters not even one word throughout the entire encounter. Instead, it is through the depth of his silence, absorbed as he was in profound meditation, that the Buddha was able to inspire one of his greatest disciples, the Bodhisattva Avalokiteshwara, to experience the revelation, and another monk, Sariputra, to provoke its explication through questioning. As Avalokiteshwara speaks, he instructs Sariputra exactly how to attain the enlightened state experienced by the Buddha.

THE HEART SUTRA

Indeed, this dialogue can be seen as a holy drama between intuitive wisdom and the rational mind, set against the backdrop of All-knowingness. That the sutra can manifest only through the joint participation of all involved brilliantly reflects the actual essence of the teaching. The sutra uses the word "emptiness"; the modern-day Vietnamese Zen master Thich Nhat Hanh calls this cosmic interplay "Interbeing"— that web of interdependency of causes and conditions that is the source of all appearance—including our very insubstantial selves.

By minutely dissecting, point by point, the elements of sentient experience, as well as the nature of all phenomena, the sutra shows exactly how the truth of "emptiness" or interdependency can be arrived at.

THE HEART SUTRA

Simply, if everything is dependent on everything else, how could there possibly be anything permanent called "me" or "mine"? And if there is no self that is neither born nor dies, how then could suffering ever possibly arise?

What is most important about the Heart Sutra is that within it lie the roots not only of ultimate wisdom but also absolute compassion. According to the Tibetan Buddhist teachings, to understand that the root of suffering lies in the delusion of the separate self is to understand that all beings suffer from that same misperception. Just as one wants to liberate him or herself, so does the path include extending that wish to be free of suffering to all beings. Indeed, the very definition of a Bodhisattva is one who

THE HEART SUTRA

delays his or her own final realization in order to help other sentient beings reach the shore of liberation.

That is the reason why the Bodhisattva Avalokiteshwara, inspired by the limitless compassion of the Buddha-mind, shared this teaching in the first place—for us, confused and suffering beings, so many centuries later.

Like the pearl inside the oyster, there is a jewel inside this sutra. The 18 sacred Sanskrit syllables of the teaching's mantra encapsulate its entire essence—exhorting *us* to go beyond anything and everything we could ever perceive or intuit.

Get caught nowhere, the mantra says, not even—and this is what is truly revolutionary for any teaching—not even in this teaching.

THE HEART SUTRA

It cannot be said enough that the full embracing of this sutra can only be brought about by one's own meditative efforts. Venerate this teaching, contemplate it, write it out by hand.

Chant the sutra loudly on awakening in the morning and chant it softly as you close your eyes at night. And, as you chant, imagine that all beings—from the smallest to the largest—are chanting with you, mining its depths, receiving its benefits, relieving the world's suffering, liberating all confusion.

Then, and only then, will this exquisite sutra begin to unfold the mysteries of its profound and sacred heart.

Pamela Bloom

Never make of Buddhism another god. Cloud not the sky-like nature of your mind with judgments, definitions, or concepts. Leave all obstacles behind and take all sentient beings with you.

THE HEART SUTRA

the Prajna Paramita

THE HEART SUTRA

༄༅། །རྒྱ་གར་སྐད་དུ། བྷ་ག་བ་ཏི་པྲཛྙཱ་པཱ་ར་མི་ཏཱ་ཧྲི་ད་ཡ།

བོད་སྐད་དུ། བཅོམ་ལྡན་འདས་མ་ཤེས་རབ་ཀྱི་ཕ་རོལ་ཏུ་ཕྱིན་པའི་སྙིང་པོ།།

བཅོམ་ལྡན་འདས་མ་ཤེས་རབ་ཀྱི་ཕ་རོལ་ཏུ་ཕྱིན་པ་ལ་ཕྱག་འཚལ་ལོ།།

འདི་སྐད་བདག་གིས་ཐོས་པ་དུས་གཅིག་ན། བཅོམ་ལྡན་འདས་རྒྱལ་པོའི་ཁབ་བྱ་རྒོད་ཕུང་པོའི་རི་ལ་དགེ་སློང་གི་དགེ་འདུན་ཆེན་པོ་དང་། བྱང་ཆུབ་སེམས་དཔའི་དགེ་འདུན་ཆེན་པོ་དང་ཐབས་གཅིག་ཏུ་བཞུགས་ཏེ། དེའི་ཚེ་བཅོམ་ལྡན་འདས་ཟབ་མོ་སྣང་བ་ཞེས་བྱ་བ་ཆོས་ཀྱི་རྣམ་གྲངས་ཀྱི་ཏིང་ངེ་འཛིན་ལ་སྙོམས་པར་བཞུགས་སོ།།

THE HEART SUTRA

In Sanskrit: Bhagavati Prajnaparamita Hrdaya

In Tibetan: Bcom Idan 'das ma shes rab kyi pha rol tu phyin pa'i snying po

Homage to the Blessed One, the Perfection of Wisdom!

Thus I heard at one time: The Blessed One was staying on the Vulture Peak in Rajagrha, together with a great assembly of monks, and a great assembly of bodhisattvas, and at that time the Blessed One was entering into the concentration of the Preaching of the Dharma called "Profound Illumination."

THE HEART SUTRA

ཡང་དེའི་ཚེ་བཅོམ་ལྡན་འདས་ཟབ་མོ་སྣང་བ་ཞེས་བྱ་བ་ཆོས་ཀྱི་རྣམ་གྲངས་ཀྱི་ཏིང་ངེ་འཛིན་ལ་སྙོམས་པར་ཞུགས་སོ། །ཡང་དེའི་ཚེ་བྱང་ཆུབ་སེམས་དཔའ་སེམས་དཔའ་ཆེན་པོ་འཕགས་པ་སྤྱན་རས་གཟིགས་དབང་ཕྱུག་ཤེས་རབ་ཀྱི་ཕ་རོལ་ཏུ་ཕྱིན་པ་ཟབ་མོ་སྤྱོད་པ་ཉིད་ལ་རྣམ་པར་བལྟ་ཞིང༌། ཕུང་པོ་ལྔ་པོ་དེ་དག་ལ་ཡང་རང་བཞིན་གྱིས་སྟོང་པར་རྣམ་པར་བལྟའོ། །

དེ་ནས་སངས་རྒྱས་ཀྱི་མཐུས། ཚེ་དང་ལྡན་པ་ཤཱ་རིའི་བུས་བྱང་ཆུབ་སེམས་དཔའ་སེམས་དཔའ་ཆེན་པོ་འཕགས་པ་སྤྱན་རས་གཟིགས་དབང་ཕྱུག་ལ་འདི་སྐད་ཅེས་སྨྲས་སོ། །

རིགས་ཀྱི་བུ་གང་ལ་ལ་ཤེས་རབ་ཀྱི་ཕ་རོལ་ཏུ་ཕྱིན་པ་ཟབ་མོ་སྤྱོད་པ་སྤྱད་པར་འདོད་པ་དེས་ཇི་ལྟར་བསླབ་པར་བྱ།

དེ་སྐད་ཅེས་སྨྲས་པ་དང༌། བྱང་ཆུབ་སེམས་དཔའ་སེམས་དཔའ་ཆེན་པོ་འཕགས་པ་སྤྱན་རས་གཟིགས་དབང་ཕྱུག་གིས་ཚེ་དང་ལྡན་པ་ཤཱ་རིའི་བུ་ལ་འདི་སྐད་ཅེས་སྨྲས་སོ། །

THE HEART SUTRA

Now, at that time the bodhisattva, mahasattva Arya Avalokiteshwara, observing the practice itself of the profound Perfection of Wisdom, observed that even those five aggregates are intrinsically empty.

Then, through the empowerment of the Buddha, the elder Sariputra spoke thus to the bodhisattva, mahasattva Arya Avalokiteshwara.

"How should whichever gentle son who desires to practice the practice of the profound Perfection of Wisdom learn it?"

He spoke thus, and the bodhisattva, mahasattva Arya Avalokiteshwara spoke thus to the elder Sardvatiputra.

THE HEART SUTRA

དེ་ནས་བྱེ་བྲག་ཏུ་སྨྲ་བའི་བུ་ཤཱ་རིའི་བུས། བྱང་ཆུབ་སེམས་དཔའ་སེམས་དཔའ་ཆེན་པོ་སྤྱན་རས་གཟིགས་དབང་ཕྱུག་ལ་འདི་སྐད་ཅེས་སྨྲས་སོ། །རིགས་ཀྱི་བུའམ་རིགས་ཀྱི་བུ་མོ་གང་ལ་ལ་ཤེས་རབ་ཀྱི་ཕ་རོལ་ཏུ་ཕྱིན་པ་ཟབ་མོ་སྤྱོད་པ་སྤྱད་པར་འདོད་པ་དེས་ཇི་ལྟར་བསླབ་པར་བྱ་སྟེ། ཕུང་པོ་ལྔ་པོ་དེ་དག་ཀྱང་རང་བཞིན་གྱིས་སྟོང་པར་རྣམ་པར་ཡང་དག་པར་རྗེས་སུ་བལྟའོ། །

གཟུགས་སྟོང་པའོ། །སྟོང་པ་ཉིད་གཟུགས་སོ། །གཟུགས་ལས་སྟོང་པ་ཉིད་གཞན་མ་ཡིན་ནོ། །སྟོང་པ་ཉིད་ལས་ཀྱང་གཟུགས་གཞན་མ་ཡིན་ནོ། དེ་བཞིན་དུ་ཚོར་བ་དང་། འདུ་ཤེས་དང་། འདུ་བྱེད་དང་། རྣམ་པར་ཤེས་པ་རྣམས་སྟོང་པའོ། །

ཤཱ་རིའི་བུ་འདི་ལྟ་བས་ན་ཆོས་ཐམས་ཅད་སྟོང་པ་ཉིད་དེ། མཚན་ཉིད་མེད་པ། མ་སྐྱེས་པ། མ་འགགས་པ། དྲི་མེད་པ། དྲི་མ་དང་བྲལ་བ་མེད་པ། བྲི་བ་མེད་པ། གང་བ་མེད་པའོ། །

THE HEART SUTRA

"Sariputra! Whichever gentle son or gentle daughter desires to practice the practice of the profound Perfection of Wisdom should observe thus, and he will behold that even those five aggregates are intrinsically empty.

Matter is empty. Emptiness is matter. Emptiness is not other than matter. Matter is also not other than emptiness. In such a way feeling, concept, disposition, and cognition are empty.

Sariputra! Therefore all elements are emptiness and without characteristic marks, non-arising, non-ceasing, without stain, without freedom from stain, without decrease, without increase.

THE HEART SUTRA

རྣ་རིའི་བུ་དེ་ལྟ་བས་ན་སྟོང་པ་ཉིད་ལ་གཟུགས་མེད། ཚོར་བ་མེད། འདུ་ཤེས་མེད། འདུ་བྱེད་རྣམས་མེད། རྣམ་པར་ཤེས་པ་མེད། མིག་མེད། རྣ་བ་མེད། སྣ་མེད། ལྕེ་མེད། ལུས་མེད། ཡིད་མེད། གཟུགས་མེད། སྒྲ་མེད། དྲི་མེད། རོ་མེད། རེག་བྱ་མེད། ཆོས་མེད་དོ།།

མིག་གི་ཁམས་མེད་པ་ནས་ཡིད་ཀྱི་ཁམས་མེད། ཡིད་ཀྱི་རྣམ་པར་ཤེས་པའི་ཁམས་ཀྱི་བར་དུ་ཡང་མེད་དོ།།

མ་རིག་པ་མེད། མ་རིག་པ་ཟད་པ་མེད་པ་ནས་རྒ་ཤི་མེད། རྒ་ཤི་ཟད་པའི་བར་དུ་ཡང་མེད་དོ།།

Sariputra! Therefore emptiness is without matter, without feeling, without concept, without disposition, without cognition, without eye, without ear, without nose, without tongue, without body, without mind, without physical form, without voice, without odor, without taste, without tactile object, without mental object.

And from: without the sense realm of the eye, even as far as: without the sense realm of the mind, without the sense realm of the mental cognition.

And from: without ignorance, without the destruction of ignorance, even as far as: without old age and death, without the destruction of old age and death.

THE HEART SUTRA

སྐྱག་བསྙལ་བ་དང་། ཀུན་འབྱུང་བ་དང་། འགོག་པ་དང་། ལམ་མེད། ཡེ་ཤེས་མེད། ཐོབ་པ་མེད། མ་ཐོབ་པ་ཡང་མེད་དོ།།

དེ་རིའི་ཕྱིར་དེ་ཤ་རིའི་བུ་བྱང་ཆུབ་སེམས་དཔའ་རྣམས་ཐོབ་པ་མེད་པའི་ཕྱིར། ཤེས་རབ་ཀྱི་ཕ་རོལ་ཏུ་ཕྱིན་པ་ལ་བརྟེན་ཅིང་གནས་ཏེ། སེམས་ལ་སྒྲིབ་པ་མེད་པས་སྐྲག་པ་མེད་དེ། ཕྱིན་ཅི་ལོག་ལས་ཤིན་ཏུ་འདས་ནས་མྱ་ངན་ལས་འདས་པའི་མཐར་ཕྱིན་ཏོ།།

དུས་གསུམ་དུ་རྣམ་པར་བཞུགས་པའི་སངས་རྒྱས་ཐམས་ཅད་ཀྱང་ཤེས་རབ་ཀྱི་ཕ་རོལ་ཏུ་ཕྱིན་པ་ལ་བརྟེན་ནས། བླ་ན་མེད་པ་ཡང་དག་པར་རྫོགས་པའི་བྱང་ཆུབ་ཏུ་མངོན་པར་རྫོགས་པར་སངས་རྒྱས་སོ།།

Without suffering, and its arisal, and its cessation, and the path, without wisdom, without attainment, and also without non-attainment.

Sariputra! Therefore because bodhisattvas are without attainment, they dwell relying on the Perfection of Wisdom, and since they are without obstruction in their minds they are without fear, and completely transcending perversity they reach the finale, which is nirvana.

All the buddhas resident throughout the three times too, having relied on the Perfection of Wisdom, fully awakened to unexcelled, perfect Awakening.

THE HEART SUTRA

དེ་ལྟ་བས་ན་ཤེས་རབ་ཀྱི་ཕ་རོལ་ཏུ་ཕྱིན་པའི་སྔགས། རིག་པ་ཆེན་པོའི་སྔགས། བླ་ན་མེད་པའི་སྔགས། མི་མཉམ་པ་དང་མཉམ་པའི་སྔགས། སྡུག་བསྔལ་ཐམས་ཅད་རབ་ཏུ་ཞི་བར་བྱེད་པའི་སྔགས། མི་བརྫུན་པས་ན་བདེན་པར་ཤེས་པར་བྱ་སྟེ། ཤེས་རབ་ཀྱི་ཕ་རོལ་ཏུ་ཕྱིན་པའི་སྔགས་སྨྲས་པ།

ཏདྱཐཱ། ཨོཾ་ག་ཏེ་ག་ཏེ་པཱ་ར་ག་ཏེ་པཱ་ར་སཾ་ག་ཏེ། བོ་དྷི་སྭཱ་ཧཱ།

ཤཱ་རིའི་བུ་བྱང་ཆུབ་སེམས་དཔའ་སེམས་དཔའ་ཆེན་པོས་དེ་ལྟར་ཤེས་རབ་ཀྱི་ཕ་རོལ་ཏུ་ཕྱིན་པ་ཟབ་མོ་ལ་བསླབ་པར་བྱའོ༎

དེ་ནས་བཅོམ་ལྡན་འདས་ཏིང་ངེ་འཛིན་དེ་ལས་བཞེངས་ཏེ། བྱང་ཆུབ་སེམས་དཔའ་སེམས་དཔའ་ཆེན་པོ་འཕགས་པ་སྤྱན་རས་གཟིགས་དབང་ཕྱུག་ལ་ལེགས་སོ་ཞེས་བྱ་བ་བྱིན་ནས། ལེགས་སོ་ལེགས་སོ༎ རིགས་ཀྱི་བུ་དེ་དེ་བཞིན་ནོ༎

26

THE HEART SUTRA

Therefore you should know that the mantra of the Perfection of Wisdom, the mantra of great knowledge, the unexcelled mantra, the mantra equal to the unequalled, the mantra which assuages all sufferings, since it is not spurious, is true, and the mantra of the Perfection of Wisdom says:

tadyatha om gate gate paragate parasamgate bodhi svaha.

Sariputra! Thus should the bodhisattva, mahasattva learn the profound Perfection of Wisdom."

Then, the Blessed One rose from that concentration and offering commendation to the bodhisattva, mahasattva Arya Avalokiteshwara said: "Well done! Well done! Gentle son, it is just so."

THE HEART SUTRA

རིགས་ཀྱི་བུ་དེ་བཞིན་ནོ། །དེ་ལྟར་སྦྱོད་ཀྱིས་བསྟན་པ་དེ་
བཞིན་དུ་ཤེས་རབ་ཀྱི་ཕ་རོལ་ཏུ་ཕྱིན་པ་ཟབ་མོ་ལ་སྤྱད་པར་བྱ་སྟེ།
དེ་བཞིན་གཤེགས་པ་རྣམས་ཀྱང་རྗེས་སུ་ཡི་རང་ངོ་། །

བཅོམ་ལྡན་འདས་ཀྱིས་དེ་སྐད་ཅེས་བཀའ་སྩལ་ནས། ཚེ་དང་
ལྡན་པ་ཤཱ་རིའི་བུ་དང་། བྱང་ཆུབ་སེམས་དཔའ་སེམས་དཔའ་ཆེན་
པོ་འཕགས་པ་སྤྱན་རས་གཟིགས་དབང་ཕྱུག་དང་། ཐམས་ཅད་
དང་ལྡན་པའི་འཁོར་དེ་དང་། ལྷ་དང་། མི་དང་། ལྷ་མ་ཡིན་
དང་། དྲི་ཟར་བཅས་པའི་འཇིག་རྟེན་ཡི་རངས་ཏེ། བཅོམ་
ལྡན་འདས་ཀྱིས་གསུངས་པ་ལ་མངོན་པར་བསྟོད་དོ། །

བཅོམ་ལྡན་འདས་མ་ཤེས་རབ་ཀྱི་ཕ་རོལ་ཏུ་ཕྱིན་པའི་སྙིང་པོ་
ཞེས་བྱ་བ་ཐེག་པ་ཆེན་པོའི་མདོ་རྫོགས་སོ། །

"Gentle son, it is just so, and just as you have stated so should one practice the profound Perfection of Wisdom, and even the Sugatas will be delighted."

The Blessed One having spoken thus, the elder Sariputra, the bodhisattva, mahasattva Arya Avalokiteshwara, the world encompassing that entire audience, and gods, and men, and asuras, and gandharvas rejoiced, and acclaimed what the Blessed One had said.

The Mahayana sutra called the Blessed Heart of the Perfection of Wisdom is concluded.

THE HEART SUTRA

about the translation

Translated by the Indian scholar Vimalmitra and the Lotsawa Dge slong Rin chen sde, this version of the Heart Sutra was revised and put in order by the chief revisor Lotsāwa Dge slong Nam mkha', and others. It was corrected by comparing it with that written on the wall of the Dge rgyas bye ma gling of the Lhun gyis grub pa monastery Sri Bsam yas.

THE HEART SUTRA

about Pamela Bloom

A student of Buddhism for over 20 years, Pamela Bloom is an award-winning writer and the author of *Buddhist Acts of Compassion* (Conari Press, 2000), a collection of true stories about the transformative power of compassion in everyday life. She is also an energy healer, an interfaith minister and intuitive counselor, specializing in the healing power of sound.

ACKNOWLEDGMENTS

Cover: Robert Beer; inset: Brian Beresford/Nomad Picture Library.

With thanks to Brighton Buddhist Centre for allowing us to photograph their Bhoddisitvas.